COUNTRY PROFILES

EL SALVADOR

BY CHRIS BOWMAN

BELLWETHER MEDIA • MINNEAPOLIS, MN

Blastoff! Discovery launches a new mission: reading to learn. Filled with facts and features, each book offers you an exciting new world to explore!

This edition first published in 2020 by Bellwether Media, Inc.

No part of this publication may be reproduced in whole or in part without written permission of the publisher.
For information regarding permission, write to Bellwether Media, Inc.,
Attention: Permissions Department,
6012 Blue Circle Drive, Minnetonka, MN 55343.

Library of Congress Cataloging-in-Publication Data

Names: Bowman, Chris, 1990- author.
Title: El Salvador / by Chris Bowman.
Description: Minneapolis, MN : Bellwether Media, Inc., 2020. |
  Series: Blastoff! Discovery: country profiles | Includes bibliographical
  references and index. | Audience: Ages: 7-13 | Audience:
  Grades: 4-6 | Summary: "Engaging images accompany
  information about El Salvador. The combination of high-interest
  subject matter and narrative text is intended for students in
  grades 3 through 8"– Provided by publisher.
Identifiers: LCCN 2019034852 (print) | LCCN 2019034853
  (ebook) | ISBN 9781644871669 (library binding) | ISBN
  9781618918420 (ebook)
Subjects: LCSH: El Salvador–Juvenile literature. | El Salvador–Social
  life and customs–Juvenile literature.
Classification: LCC F1483.2 .B69 2020 (print) | LCC F1483.2
  (ebook) | DDC 972.84–dc23
LC record available at https://lccn.loc.gov/2019034852
LC ebook record available at https://lccn.loc.gov/2019034853

Editor: Rebecca Sabelko   Designer: Brittany McIntosh

Printed in the United States of America, North Mankato, MN.

TABLE OF CONTENTS

THE HIDDEN PYRAMID	4
LOCATION	6
LANDSCAPE AND CLIMATE	8
WILDLIFE	10
PEOPLE	12
COMMUNITIES	14
CUSTOMS	16
SCHOOL AND WORK	18
PLAY	20
FOOD	22
CELEBRATIONS	24
TIMELINE	26
EL SALVADOR FACTS	28
GLOSSARY	30
TO LEARN MORE	31
INDEX	32

THE HIDDEN PYRAMID

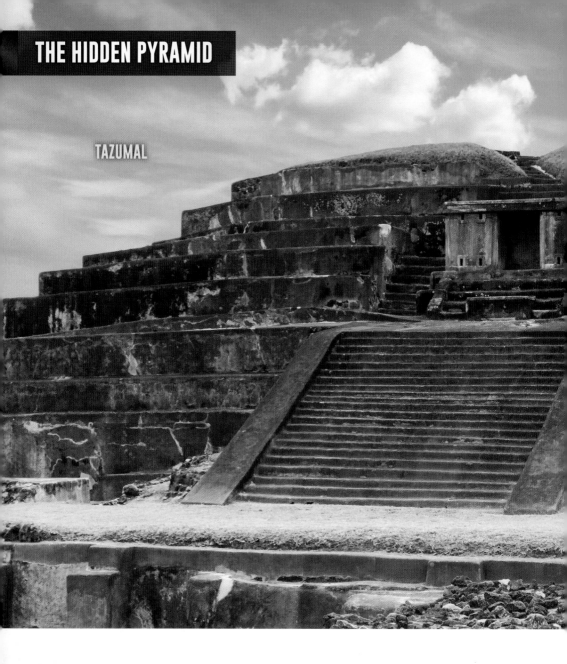

TAZUMAL

A family arrives in the small town of Chalchuapa in western El Salvador. They venture to the country's largest Mayan ruins, Tazumal, found tucked behind shops and restaurants. The family is amazed by this great pyramid that reaches about 75 feet (23 meters) into the sky!

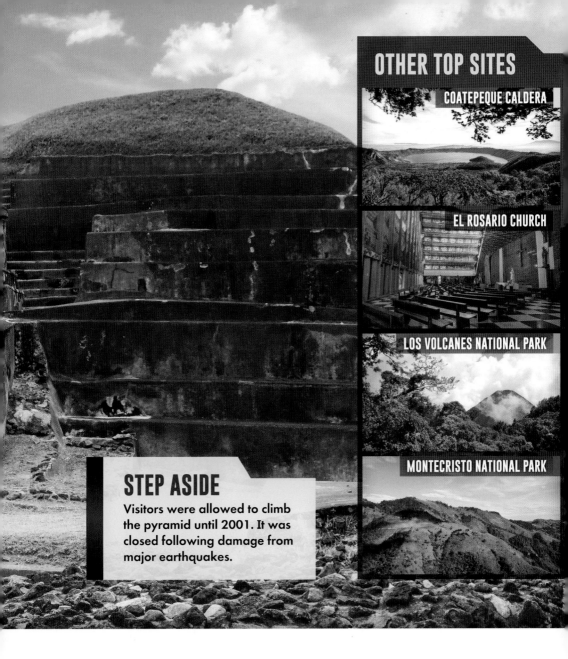

OTHER TOP SITES

COATEPEQUE CALDERA

EL ROSARIO CHURCH

LOS VOLCANES NATIONAL PARK

MONTECRISTO NATIONAL PARK

STEP ASIDE

Visitors were allowed to climb the pyramid until 2001. It was closed following damage from major earthquakes.

Then the family visits the museum to learn about the history of Tazumal. The ruins date back to 100 CE and were abandoned around 1200 CE. They learn about all the **tombs**, jewelry, and pottery found within the ruins. In this small neighborhood, El Salvador's history is on display!

El Salvador is the smallest country in Central America. This short, wide country covers 8,124 square miles (21,041 square kilometers). Its capital, San Salvador, rests in the *Valle de las Hamacas*, or Valley of the Hammocks, in west-central El Salvador.

El Salvador is the only country in Central America that does not have a border with the Caribbean Sea. El Salvador's neighbor to the northwest is Guatemala. It shares a long border with Honduras to the north and east. The shores of the Pacific Ocean span El Salvador's southern edge.

GUATEMALA

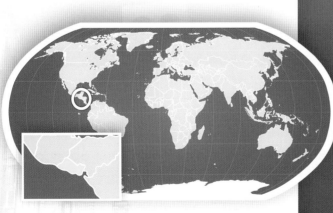

HONDURAS

SANTA ANA

MEJICANOS

SOYAPANGO

SAN MIGUEL

EL SALVADOR

SAN SALVADOR

PACIFIC
OCEAN

El Salvador is divided into three main landscapes. The Sierra Madre Mountains line the northern border with Honduras. The central part of the country is filled with green valleys and **plateaus**. There are also many **volcanoes**. The coastal lowlands in the south are a thin, **fertile** stretch that lines the Pacific Ocean.

= SIERRA MADRE MOUNTAINS
= COASTAL LOWLANDS

N
W + E
S

EL ZONTE REGION

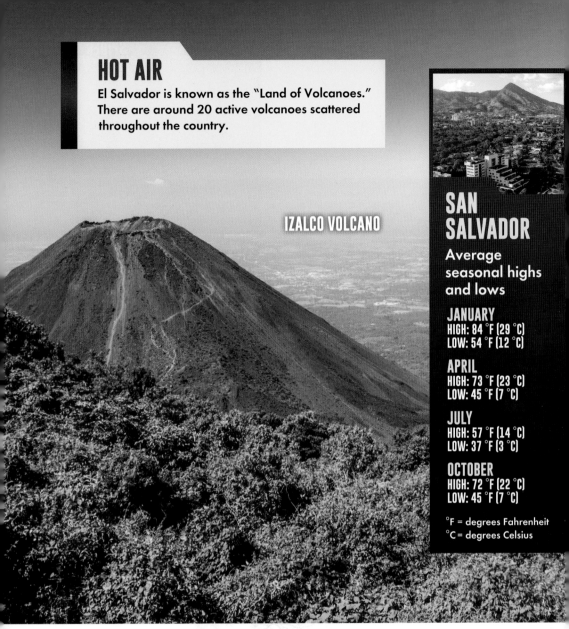

HOT AIR

El Salvador is known as the "Land of Volcanoes." There are around 20 active volcanoes scattered throughout the country.

IZALCO VOLCANO

SAN SALVADOR

Average seasonal highs and lows

JANUARY
HIGH: 84 °F (29 °C)
LOW: 54 °F (12 °C)

APRIL
HIGH: 73 °F (23 °C)
LOW: 45 °F (7 °C)

JULY
HIGH: 57 °F (14 °C)
LOW: 37 °F (3 °C)

OCTOBER
HIGH: 72 °F (22 °C)
LOW: 45 °F (7 °C)

°F = degrees Fahrenheit
°C = degrees Celsius

The weather along El Salvador's southern **plains** is usually warmer than areas higher up in the mountains. The country's rainy season is known as *invierno*. It lasts from May to October. The dry summer runs from November to April.

WILDLIFE

El Salvador lost many of its forests in the 1900s. This led to fewer animals living there. However, spider monkeys still live among the trees. Margays hunt small animals such as rats, squirrels, and opossums. Iguanas and armadillos live near the coast.

The country is known for its birds and butterflies. Turquoise-browed motmots are colorful birds found all over El Salvador. Toucans, quetzals, and parakeets also fly overhead. Zebra longwings and hundreds of other butterfly species fill the skies.

SPIDER MONKEY

MARGAY

IGUANA

ZEBRA LONGWING

ARMADILLO

TURQUOISE-BROWED
MOTMOT

TURQUOISE-BROWED MOTMOT

Life Span: unknown

Red List Status: least concern

turquoise-browed motmot range = ■

LEAST CONCERN	NEAR THREATENED	VULNERABLE	ENDANGERED	CRITICALLY ENDANGERED	EXTINCT IN THE WILD	EXTINCT

Most people living in El Salvador are *mestizos*. They have both European and **native** backgrounds. A smaller number of people have only European **ancestors**. Spanish ancestors are the most common. El Salvador's biggest native population is Pipil.

The official language of El Salvador is Spanish. But a small number of native communities still speak their own language of Nawat. About half of all Salvadorans belong to the Roman Catholic Church. El Salvador also has a growing number of Protestant Christians.

FAMOUS FACE

Name: Mauricio Cienfuegos
Birthday: February 12, 1968
Hometown: San Salvador, El Salvador
Famous for: An early star in Major League Soccer, he played in seven all-star games and won many awards including the MLS Cup, Most Valuable Player, and Humanitarian of the Year

SPEAK SPANISH

ENGLISH	SPANISH	HOW TO SAY IT
hello	hola	OH-lah
goodbye	adiós	ah-dee-OHS
please	por favor	pohr fah-VOR
thank you	gracias	grah-SEE-ahs
yes	sí	SEE
no	no	noh

SAN SALVADOR

COMMUNITIES

In the cities, many people live in apartments and townhouses. Wealthy Salvadorans often have large single-family homes. Lower-income families usually live in older buildings and shacks. Recent natural disasters have damaged many buildings. This has led to overcrowding in many cities.

EL TUNCO

Many **rural** Salvadorans live in small **adobe** houses. These often have dirt floors and **thatched roofs**. Few Salvadorans own cars. Most people walk or take the bus to get around. Taxis are also common around the city streets.

15

CUSTOMS

FRIENDLY HELLO

Salvadorans greet each other with *buenos días* in the morning, *buenas tardes* in the afternoon, and *buenas noches* in the evening. Many Salvadorans shorten this greeting to *buenas* throughout the day.

Friends and family are very important to Salvadorans. Large families often live together. It is also common for friends and family to regularly stop by without making plans ahead of time. These visits keep their bonds strong.

Music plays a central role in many Salvadorans' daily lives. Salvadoran folk music, or *canción popular*, often floats through the air in restaurants and other public places. Another kind of **traditional** music is *cumbia*. It is a favorite for people of all ages in El Salvador. Recently, dance music called *reggaetón* has grown popular among many young Salvadorans.

Children in El Salvador begin school at age 7 and continue with nine years of primary school. Students then go on to secondary school, where they can pick topics to study. Depending on what they choose, secondary school lasts either two or three years.

Over half of all Salvadorans work in **service jobs**. Many of these are in **tourism**, as the country's ancient ruins attract many visitors. Farmers in El Salvador are known for their coffee and cotton. Other major **exports** are corn and sugar. People also **manufacture** products such as canned foods and electronics.

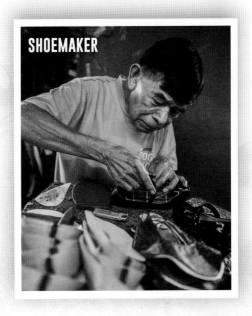

SHOEMAKER

FARMER

19

SOCCER

Soccer is the national sport of El Salvador. Salvadorans enjoy cheering for the country's many club teams. They also play pick-up matches in parks or other open spaces. Basketball is another favorite sport. Baseball and boxing are growing more popular.

BASKETBALL

Salvadorans love to spend time outside. Many families go on vacation to the Pacific Ocean, where they relax by surfing, fishing, and kayaking. People also enjoy visiting the country's mountains and volcanoes. El Salvador has many great parks and hiking trails to enjoy.

SURFING

FERNANDO LLORT ART

Fernando Llort is often called "El Salvador's National Artist." Make your own art in Llort's bright, simple style!

What You Need:
- paper
- a pencil
- a black marker
- paint or markers

What You Do:
1. Using a pencil and paper, draw simple pictures of animals, plants, buildings, and people.
2. When you are happy with the drawings, trace them with your black marker.
3. Using bright paints or markers, color in your drawings.

NATIONAL TREASURE

Pupusas are considered the national dish of El Salvador. They can be eaten as a snack or during breakfast, lunch, or dinner.

Salvadorans start their day with a hearty breakfast. Beans, eggs, cheese, tortillas, and plantains are common. People may also enjoy *pupusas*, corn tortillas stuffed with beans, meat, and cheese. Lunch and dinner may include *empanadas*, or pastries filled with meat, potatoes, and cheese. Pockets of corn dough stuffed with meat and corn called *tamales* are also enjoyed.

Salvadorans often enjoy sweet treats. On warm days, people sip *ensalada*, a refreshing juice filled with small pieces of fruit. *Tres leches*, or cake made with three types of milk, and *pastelitos*, small pastries filled with custard or jam, are favorite desserts.

EMPANADAS

TRES LECHES

ENSALADA

Ingredients:
1 20-ounce can of pineapple chunks
   with juice
2 apples
2 oranges
1 mango
juice from one lemon or lime
juice from one orange
8 cups water
1/4 cup sugar
pinch of salt

Steps:
1. Have an adult help you peel and chop the fruits into small pieces.

2. Place the chopped pineapple, apples, oranges, and mango into a large mixing bowl.

3. Add the pineapple, orange, and lemon juices to the bowl.

4. Add the sugar and salt and stir well.

5. Let the mixture sit for a half hour.

6. Pour the mixture and the water into a large pitcher and stir well.

7. Place the pitcher in the refrigerator for one hour, then enjoy!

CELEBRATIONS

Salvadorans are known for their colorful religious festivals. Most towns have a large celebration for their **patron saint**. The biggest of these is San Salvador's *El Salvador del Mundo*, or "the Savior of the World." Dancers in bright costumes and large floats fill the streets during this weeklong festival in August.

The week of Easter, or *Semana Santa*, is an important holiday in El Salvador. The streets are covered with colorful *alfombras*, or carpets, made of flowers or sawdust. Christmas celebrations often begin with church on Christmas Eve. Then families eat tamales and set off fireworks. Salvadorans love to celebrate with friends and family!

SEMANA SANTA ALFOMBRA

SHARING THE DAY

El Salvador, Costa Rica, Guatemala, Honduras, and Nicaragua all celebrate Independence Day on September 15. This is the day they became free from Spain!

INDEPENDENCE DAY

TIMELINE

8000 BCE
The first people move to the area now called El Salvador

1823
El Salvador joins the United Provinces of Central America

1821
El Salvador becomes independent from Spain

1524 CE
Spanish explorer Pedro de Alvarado reaches El Salvador

1840
El Salvador gains full independence after the United Provinces of Central America falls

1961
The armed forces overthrow the government, leading to 30 years of unrest and violence

2009
Powerful mudslides and heavy flooding leave trails of destruction throughout the country

2001
Deadly earthquakes cause widespread damage throughout El Salvador

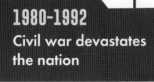

1980-1992
Civil war devastates the nation

2005
The Ilamatepec volcano erupts

EL SALVADOR FACTS

Official Name: Republic of El Salvador

Flag of El Salvador: El Salvador's flag has three horizontal bands. The bands on the top and bottom are solid blue, which represent the Pacific Ocean and the Caribbean Sea. The white middle band stands for the land in between as well as peace and prosperity. The country's coat of arms is in the middle of the flag.

Area: 8,124 square miles (21,041 square kilometers)

Capital City: San Salvador

Important Cities: Soyapango, Santa Ana, San Miguel, Mejicanos

Population: 6,187,271 (July 2018)

WHERE PEOPLE LIVE

COUNTRYSIDE
27.3%

CITY
72.7%

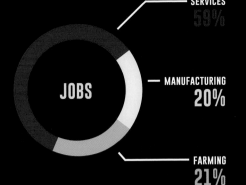

SERVICES
59%

JOBS

MANUFACTURING
20%

FARMING
21%

Main Exports:

coffee

sugar

textiles

chemicals

paper

machines

National Holiday:
Independence Day (September 15)

Main Language:
Spanish

Form of Government:
presidential republic

Title for Country Leader:
president

RELIGION

PROTESTANT
36%

OTHER
2%

NONE
12%

ROMAN
CATHOLIC
50%

Unit of Money:
U.S. dollar

GLOSSARY

adobe—a building material made of mud and straw

ancestors—relatives who lived long ago

exports—products sold by one country to another

fertile—able to support growth

manufacture—to make products, often with machines

native—originally from the area or related to a group of people that began in the area

patron saint—a saint who is believed to look after a country or group of people

plains—large areas of flat land

plateaus—areas of flat, raised land

rural—related to the countryside

service jobs—jobs that perform tasks for people or businesses

thatched roofs—roofs with coverings made of grass or straw

tombs—buildings for burying the dead

tourism—the business of people traveling to visit other places

traditional—related to customs, ideas, or beliefs handed down from one generation to the next

volcanoes—holes in the earth; when a volcano erupts, hot ash, gas, or melted rock called lava shoots out.

TO LEARN MORE

AT THE LIBRARY

Foley, Erin, Rafiz Hapipi, and Debbie Nevins.
El Salvador. New York, N.Y.: Cavendish Square
Publishing, 2016.

Green, Sara. *Ancient Maya*. Minneapolis, Minn.:
Bellwether Media, 2020.

Shields, Charles J. *El Salvador*. Philadelphia, Pa.:
Mason Crest, 2016.

ON THE WEB

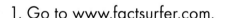

FACTSURFER

Factsurfer.com gives you
a safe, fun way to find
more information.

1. Go to www.factsurfer.com.

2. Enter "El Salvador" into the search box
   and click Q.

3. Select your book cover to see a list
   of related web sites.

INDEX

activities, 21

capital (see San Salvador)

celebrations, 24-25

Christmas, 24

Cienfuegos, Mauricio, 13

climate, 9

communities, 14-15

customs, 16-17

education, 18

El Salvador del Mundo, 24

fast facts, 28-29

Fernando Llort art (activity), 21

food, 22-23, 24

housing, 14, 15

Independence Day, 25

landmarks, 4, 5

landscape, 8-9, 10

language, 13

location, 6-7

music, 17

people, 12-13

recipe, 23

religion, 13, 24

San Salvador, 6, 7, 9, 13,
    14, 24

Semana Santa, 24

size, 6

sports, 20

Tazumal, 4-5

timeline, 26-27

transportation, 15

wildlife, 10-11

work, 19